ESSENTIAL ENERGY

NUCLEAR ENERGY

Robert Snedden

Heinemann Library
Chicago, Illinois

© 2002, 2006 Heinemann Library
a division of Reed Elsevier Inc.
Chicago, Illinois

Customer Service 888-454-2279
Visit our website at www.heinemannraintree.com

Designed by David Poole and Damco Solutions Ltd
Illustrations by Jeff Edwards
Printed and bound by WKT Company Ltd in China

10 09 08 07 06
10 9 8 7 6 5 4 3 2 1

New edition ISBN: 1 4034 8734 0 (hardback)
                 1 4034 8739 1 (paperback)

The Library of Congress has cataloged the first edition as follows:
Snedden, Robert.
   Nuclear energy / by Robert Snedden.
      p. cm. -- (Essential energy)
Includes bibliographical references and index.
   ISBN 1-57572-444-8 (lib. bdg.)
   1. Nuclear energy -- Juvenile literature. [1. Nuclear energy.] I. Title.
   QC792.5 .S54 2001
   333.792'4 -- dc21
                                                                    00-013239

Acknowledgments
The publishers would like to thank the following for permission to reproduce photographs: Camera Press: p. 13; Corbis: pp. 5, 11, 14, 28; Environmental Images: pp. 4, 22, 24, 30, 31, 36; Landauer: p. 34; Popperfoto: pp. 39, 42, 43; Robert Harding Picture Library: p. 18; Science Photo Library: pp. 8, 12, 15, 17, 20, 23, 25, 26, 27, 29, 32, 33, 37, 41.

Cover photograph of a nuclear explosion reproduced with permission of Corbis.

The publishers would like to thank Helen Lloyd for her assistance in the preparation of this book.

Any words appearing in the text in bold, **like this,** are explained in the glossary.

CONTENTS

NUCLEAR POWER?
NO THANKS!

At the beginning of the 20th century, no one dreamed that there could be such a thing as nuclear power. Scientists were just beginning to discover **radioactivity** and taking their first steps toward discovering how **atoms**, the particles from which all matter is made, are put together. In 1905 Albert Einstein, in his theory of relativity, showed that **mass** could be changed into energy, and vice versa. By 1918 Sir Ernest Rutherford had shown that atoms could be split. By 1942 the world had its first nuclear **reactor**.

In the late 20th century, nuclear power was one of the biggest sources of energy for the industrialized world, second only to **fossil fuels**. For many people, **nuclear energy** was the answer to the problem of dwindling fossil fuel resources and to the pollution caused by burning fossil fuels. Many people thought that nuclear power would soon provide incredibly cheap electricity. But today, the nuclear industry has stopped growing. Germany, for example, announced in June 2000 that it would phase out all its nuclear power plants. Many other countries, including Austria, Italy, and the Philippines, have done the same. So, what is wrong with nuclear power?

■ Anti-nuclear protestors demonstrated for a month
against the Superphénix reactor in France.

Reactor reactions

Many people are concerned about the environmental and health problems related to nuclear power. Nuclear reactors produce **radiation**, which is harmful to living things. High doses of radiation can kill very quickly. Small doses, such as what might leak from a normally operating nuclear plant, could build up over many years and also cause damage. However, with or without nuclear power, radiation is a fact of life. It comes from the Sun, from rocks, from medical X-rays, and even from television sets. Some scientists estimate that the average person gets five times as much radiation in a lifetime from sitting in front of the television or a computer monitor as he or she would from living near a nuclear power station.

Many people also object to nuclear power because of its possible use in nuclear weapons. Also, accidents, such as fires or explosions, could cause **radioactive** materials to be released inside a power station or even to spread outside. Government regulators in the United States have estimated that there is about a 50 percent chance of a core **meltdown** in a U.S. reactor within a twenty-year period. Disposing of the dangerous waste that is the by-product of nuclear power is also a problem.

■ Many people are afraid of living near nuclear reactors because of the possibility of accidents.

INSIDE THE ATOM

To understand how nuclear power works, we first have to take a look at the way atoms are put together. Atoms are the tiny particles from which all the materials around you are made. An atom can be divided into two parts. First, there is an outer cloud of tiny particles called **electrons**. The number of electrons in the outermost part of this cloud determines how the atom will react with other atoms in chemical reactions.

The inner part of the atom is called the **nucleus**. This consists of a tightly packed cluster of particles called **protons** and **neutrons**. Each **element** has a different number of protons and neutrons. Elements range in complexity from hydrogen, which is the simplest element and has a single proton, to uranium, which is used as a nuclear fuel and can have 235 or more protons and neutrons. Some elements can have even more particles in their nuclei. The atoms of a particular element all have the same number of protons in their nuclei. This is called the **atomic number**. The protons and neutrons take no part in chemical reactions.

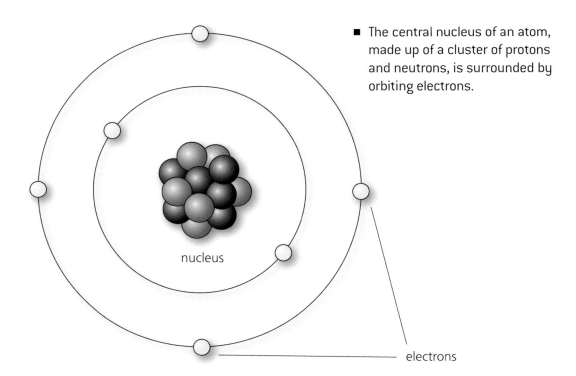

■ The central nucleus of an atom, made up of a cluster of protons and neutrons, is surrounded by orbiting electrons.

nucleus

electrons

Isotopes

It is possible for two or more atoms to have the same atomic number (the same number of protons). This means they are the same element, but they have different numbers of neutrons. Such atoms are called **isotopes** of that element. Isotopes may be stable or radioactive, and they may be naturally occurring or made in a laboratory. For example, carbon has the isotopes C12 (which is stable) and C14 (which is radioactive). The term *isotope* was coined by English chemist Frederick Soddy, who was a pioneer researcher in atomic disintegration.

Radioactive elements

Of the known elements, 92 occur in nature. These elements have atomic numbers ranging from 1 (hydrogen) to 92 (uranium). Of these elements, 81 are stable; all the others are radioactive. The radioactive elements include technetium (atomic number 43); promethium (number 61); and all the elements from polonium (number 84) up to uranium (number 92).

A radioactive substance is one in which the nuclei of its atoms are unstable. They break apart, giving out energy as they do so. When the nucleus breaks up, or **decays**, it forms a nucleus that is more stable than it was before. The new nucleus may have fewer protons than the original, which means that it has become a different element. A radioactive element may go through several stages of decay before finally becoming a stable element.

HALF-LIFE

There is no way to predict when any one radioactive nucleus will decay. However, it is possible to say that half of the atoms in a particular sample of a radioactive material will have decayed by a certain time. This is called the radioactive element's **half-life**. Each radioactive isotope has a different half-life. These can range from a tiny fraction of a second to billions of years. The half-life of uranium 238 is about the same as the age Earth is now—4.5 billion years—whereas that of polonium 213 is just over four millionths of a second.

ENERGY FROM THE ATOM

An element is a substance that cannot be split chemically into simpler substances. Elements can react together in chemical reactions. All chemical reactions involve the release or the taking up of **chemical energy**. For instance, when coal is burned, the carbon in the coal combines with oxygen to become carbon dioxide, and energy is released as heat. The atoms involved in a chemical reaction remain unchanged.

In contrast, the elements involved in a nuclear reaction can change as a result of it. In a nuclear reaction, an unstable atomic nucleus breaks up, or decays. As it does so, it releases radioactivity in the form of alpha, beta, and **gamma radiation**. A large, unstable nucleus can also release neutrons as it decays.

Missing mass

No mass is ever lost when a chemical reaction takes place. The mass of the atoms present before the reaction will always equal the mass after the reaction. However, if you add up the mass of all the particles formed by the decay of an unstable nucleus, you will find that it is less than the mass of the original nucleus. So, where is the missing mass?

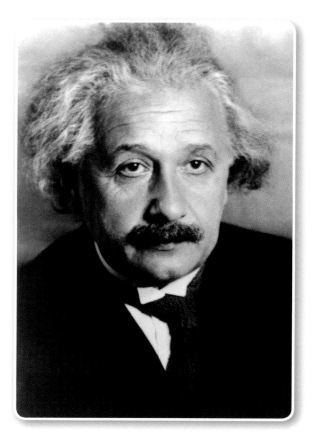

$E = mc^2$

As part of his theory of relativity, Albert Einstein showed that mass (m) and energy (E) were related by the equation $E = mc^2$, where c = the speed of light. In a nuclear reaction, mass is converted into energy. The Sun, for example, produces an enormous amount of energy from nuclear reactions in its core that change hydrogen into helium. In the process, the Sun loses over 4 million tons of mass every second!

■ In his theory of relativity, Albert Einstein (1879–1955) revealed the connection between matter and energy.

Every time a nucleus breaks apart, energy is released. In fact, the amount of energy released is massive. A given mass of uranium can provide 2.5 million times more energy than would be obtained by burning the same mass of carbon.

Most of the energy is in the form of **kinetic energy** as the nucleus flies apart. This is rapidly converted into **heat energy** as the fragments of the nucleus collide with other atoms. It is this heat that is used to generate electricity in a nuclear power station. Some of the remaining energy is carried off in the form of radioactive decay.

RADIOACTIVE DECAY

When the nucleus of a radioactive element breaks down, it can give off different types of radioactivity:

- **Alpha particles** (α) are made up of two protons and two neutrons. This is the same as the nucleus of a helium atom. They are fast moving but can be stopped by a sheet of paper and will not travel far through the air.
- **Beta particles** (β) are fast-moving electrons. They are more difficult to stop than alpha particles but can be halted by a thin sheet of metal.
- Gamma rays (γ) are not particles; they are a form of electromagnetic radiation with a very short wavelength and therefore a lot of energy. Gamma radiation is not easy to stop. A thick sheet of lead is needed to block gamma rays.

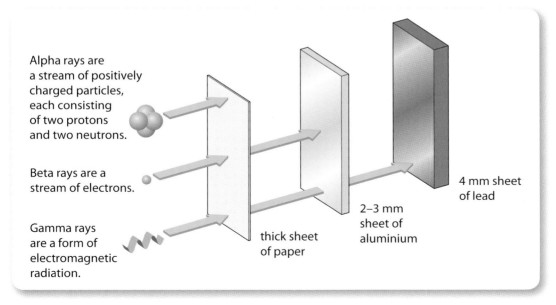

Alpha rays are a stream of positively charged particles, each consisting of two protons and two neutrons.

Beta rays are a stream of electrons.

Gamma rays are a form of electromagnetic radiation.

thick sheet of paper

2–3 mm sheet of aluminium

4 mm sheet of lead

■ Radioactive atoms can pass through other materials.

NEUTRONS AND CHAIN REACTIONS

Naturally occurring uranium contains two isotopes: U238, which makes up 99.28 percent, and U235, which makes up the other 0.72 percent. Uranium 235 is a **fissile material**. This means that if a U235 nucleus is struck by a neutron, it will **fission**, or break apart. Neutrons striking U238 nuclei will simply be scattered. As the U235 nucleus breaks apart, it releases energy and two or three more neutrons, which can then break up more U235 nuclei. These neutrons travel at around 12,400 miles (20,000 kilometers) per second—about 25,000 times faster than a space shuttle orbiting Earth! Because these neutrons can set off a **chain reaction**, they make it possible to get a continuous supply of energy from uranium.

■ This shows the fission of a uranium atom.

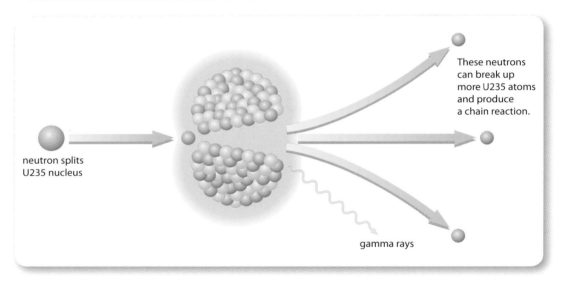

These neutrons can break up more U235 atoms and produce a chain reaction.

neutron splits U235 nucleus

gamma rays

Chain reactions

In a chain reaction, the neutrons released by the fissioning uranium will strike other nuclei. When they strike U235 nuclei, these will fission, too, releasing still more neutrons. These neutrons can go on to strike yet more nuclei, which will release yet more neutrons, and so the reaction continues. To increase the chances of neutrons striking U235, the uranium used in nuclear power stations is enriched. This makes the U235 content greater than it is normally.

There is no single chain reaction taking place. Within a typical nuclear power station, there may be about 100 million billion fission chain reactions taking place at any time.

The new nuclei formed when an unstable nucleus decays are called fission products. A uranium 235 atom becomes an atom of xenon and an atom of strontium. These new atoms are themselves unstable and will decay further.

The rate at which chain reactions take place can be controlled by introducing neutron-absorbing materials, such as **boron**, into the reactor. The fewer neutrons there are flying around, the fewer fissions there will be. Nuclear reactors use control rods to raise and lower the power output of the reactor.

■ The power of the atom is unleashed in the first detonation of an atomic bomb.

CRITICAL MASS

Neutrons reaching the surface of a reactor core can leak out, rather than trigger further fissions. The smaller the core, the greater the proportion of neutrons that leak out. The minimum amount of a fissile material that can maintain a continuous chain reaction is known as the critical mass. A reactor in which continuous chain reactions are taking place is said to be critical. If the amount of fissile material is much above the critical mass, the reaction may accelerate uncontrollably. This is called a supercritical system. This is what happens in a nuclear explosion.

UNLOCKING THE ATOM

In the early part of the 20th century, a number of researchers around the world were investigating what happens when neutrons strike uranium atoms. In 1938 German scientists Otto Hahn and Fritz Strassmann showed that when uranium is bombarded with neutrons, new, lighter elements are formed. A year later, Lise Meitner and Otto Frisch coined the term *fission* to describe this process. They showed that when the uranium was struck by neutrons, it split, or fissioned, into lighter elements.

Developing weapons

The outbreak of World War II (1939–45) led people to explore the uses of fission as a source of energy, particularly in the creation of weapons. The development of a weapon required not only that a self-sustaining fission reaction could be created, but also that a sufficient quantity of fissionable material could be produced for use in a weapon.

The U.S. government poured a huge amount of money and resources into what was named the Manhattan Project. A team lead by Enrico Fermi succeeded in making the first self-sustaining, or critical, nuclear reactor at the University of Chicago on December 2, 1942. The reactor used natural uranium embedded in graphite blocks as its fuel.

■ The world's second nuclear reactor was built at the Argonne Forest laboratory in Chicago in 1943.

As we have seen, only the U235 isotope fissions, and natural uranium only contains 0.7 percent of U235. To make a bomb, much higher concentrations of U235 are necessary. Part of the Manhattan Project's aim was to develop a way of separating U235 from U238. The solution was gaseous diffusion. You can read more about this technique on page 16.

Another way to develop weapons is to use a different fissile nucleus. An isotope of plutonium, Pu239, is formed when U238 reacts with neutrons to produce U239. The U239 then decays in two steps to produce Pu239. This Pu239 can be used in the manufacture of weapons. Once Fermi had demonstrated that a reactor could be built, the focus turned to building reactors that produce plutonium. The first such reactor was constructed in Oak Ridge, Tennessee. It took less than three years to develop this new technology. It prepared the way for the development of nuclear energy for commercial use.

"Atoms for Peace"

The **Atomic Energy** Commission (AEC) was set up in 1946 to oversee nonmilitary uses of nuclear power in the United States. In December 1953, in a speech at the United Nations, President Dwight D. Eisenhower announced his

decision to make nuclear-related information available to other countries, in order to develop peaceful uses for nuclear energy. He called this "atoms for peace." The first international conference on nuclear energy was held in Geneva, Switzerland, in 1955. Great Britain began production of nuclear-fueled electricity in 1956. The first Soviet nuclear power plant came on line in 1954, and the French began construction of their first commercial plants in 1957. By the early 1960s, nuclear power was firmly established as a commercial energy source.

■ President Eisenhower supported the use of nuclear power for peaceful, domestic uses such as the production of electricity.

URANIUM MINING

The first stage in the nuclear fuel process is the mining of uranium ore, the rock in which uranium is found. Uranium is one of the less common elements, although it is about twenty times more common than a precious metal such as silver. Mining takes place at sites where the concentration of uranium is greater than about 0.04 percent. Below this, it would cost too much to remove the uranium.

Uranium is usually found as uraninite, an **oxide** of uranium also known as pitchblende. The uranium is separated by first crushing the rock and then treating it with chemicals. The uranium leaves the mine as "yellowcake," or uranium concentrate, which is another oxide of uranium. Since the uranium concentrations are generally very low, a lot of waste is produced when uranium is removed from its ore. Even a high-concentration ore will still contain only about 1 percent uranium. For every U.S. ton of ore processed, 1,980 pounds (898 kilograms) is waste.

HOW MUCH URANIUM?

Like fossil fuels, uranium is a nonrenewable resource. There is only a limited amount available. However, how long it will last is influenced by a number of factors. For example, the use of uranium will decline if nuclear power is gradually phased out. If this happens, the reserves will last for considerably longer. Another possibililty is that the uranium currently stored in nuclear weapons could become available for power generation if these weapons were taken out of use.

■ This uranium mine is in Australia.

The risks of mining

Uranium is radioactive. Radioactivity poses health dangers for people exposed to high levels of it. All of the various isotopes that uranium forms as it decays will be present in the ore. Because these are different elements, they will be chemically different from uranium and so will form part of the waste material. The waste products left behind after the uranium has been removed, called tailings, can be covered with earth or returned underground to reduce the risk of radiation exposure.

One of these wastes is a radioactive isotope of the gas radon. This is released from the waste material. If it is inhaled, it can cause damage to the inside of the lungs as it decays. In underground uranium mines, radon tends to accumulate. Miners used to call the lung diseases they developed from breathing radioactive dust "mountain sickness."

Cutting the risks, raising the costs

Miners exposed to the average dose of radiation in a mine are six times more likely to develop lung cancer than other people. The Union of Concerned Scientists, based in the United States, says that radon levels can be reduced simply by allowing more air into the mines. They estimated that the cost of bringing exposure down to reasonably safe levels would be between 10 and 20 percent of the value of the uranium mined.

■ This is a sample of uranium 235, the fuel for nuclear reactors.

Unfortunately, spending money to do this would cut down on the amount of money the mine would make, unless the mine owner raises the selling price of the uranium the mine produces. Power stations buy their uranium from the cheapest source they can find. Because of this, they discourage mines from taking steps to increase safety. For many miners, working in mines may be risky, but it is better than no work at all.

PRODUCING NUCLEAR FUELS

Yellowcake is the raw material for nuclear fuel production. Basically, it is impure uranium trioxide that, when purified, it is a free-flowing orange-yellow powder. After it is purified, the uranium trioxide is heated in a stream of hydrogen gas at a temperature of 1,202 °F (650 °C). This produces chocolate-brown uranium dioxide. A couple of reactor types can use uranium in this form as a fuel, but most use uranium dioxide that has been enriched to contain a higher proportion of U235.

Enriching uranium

There are two ways to enrich uranium. In both methods, the uranium dioxide is heated with hydrogen fluoride gas to give lime-green uranium tetrafluoride. This is heated in fluorine gas to give uranium hexafluoride gas.

Gas diffusion

The first method relies on the fact that lighter **molecules** of a gas will **diffuse** through a **porous** material faster than heavier molecules. This means that molecules of uranium hexafluoride that contain U235 atoms will diffuse faster than molecules containing the heavier U238 atoms. This process has to be repeated many times before the uranium becomes significantly enriched. After being passed once through the porous material, it may only be 1.004 times richer in U235 than before. This method requires a great deal of energy.

FUEL PRODUCTION RISKS

The biggest risks of nuclear fuel production come not from possible exposure to radiation, but from the chemicals used in the fuel processing. Fluorine and hydrogen fluoride are extremely dangerous chemicals. Fluorine, in fact, is the most reactive of all chemicals, and both it and hydrogen fluoride can cause severe burns if they come into contact with unprotected skin. Hydrofluoric acid, a solution of hydrogen fluoride in water, penetrates deep into the skin tissues. However, it may be several hours before pain develops and the destruction of the tissues begins.

■ This gas diffusion nuclear fuel enrichment
  plant is in Paducah, Kentucky.

Gas centrifuge enrichment

The preferred method of uranium enrichment is a second method. In this
process, the uranium hexafluoride is spun in a cylinder at around 1,000
revolutions per second. Molecules containing U238 tend to move toward the
wall of the container more readily. This leaves the lighter U235 molecules in
the center. This separation is far from perfect, however, because gas molecules
are always on the move and tend to mix again. However, gas removed from
the center will be richer in U235 by between 1.05 and 1.3 times, which is an
improvement on 1.004! An enrichment plant will have a sequence of stages,
called an enrichment cascade, and will have several hundred cascades running
at the same time. Once the uranium hexafluoride has been enriched, it is
converted back into uranium dioxide by heating it with hydrogen and steam.

Gas centrifuge enrichment plants are smaller and less expensive to operate
than gas diffusion plants. Enriched uranium dioxide provides the fuel for most
of the world's nuclear reactors.

INSIDE A NUCLEAR POWER STATION

Many of the features of a nuclear power station are similar to those of other power stations. A source of fuel, such as coal, gas, or oil in a fossil fuel station, is used to provide energy to heat water. This produces high-energy steam to spin a **turbine**. The mechanical energy of the turbine is used to generate electricity. The steam is turned back into liquid water and recycled to the steam generator.

The reactor core

The heart of a nuclear power station is the reactor core. This is where the nuclear fuel is held and where it undergoes fission to produce energy. The fuel is in the form of a stack of pellets or a cylindrical rod held in a thin-walled metal container called **cladding**. The rods and cladding together are called **fuel rods**. In most reactors, a fuel element consists of several fuel rods bundled together with spaces between them through which **coolants** can flow. There will be 200 or more fuel elements in a typical reactor. A fuel element will produce energy for three to six years before it has to be replaced.

■ A worker changes fuel rods in a nuclear power station in Switzerland.

Coolants

The gas or liquid coolant passes through the reactor core and carries the heat away to the steam generators. The coolant comes into contact with the cladding, but not directly with the nuclear fuel. A coolant has to be selected carefully. It must not react chemically with the cladding. It must not absorb too many neutrons, because this would slow down the chain reaction. It should also be inexpensive. The majority of reactors use carbon dioxide, helium gases, and light and heavy water. Light water is everyday water; heavy water has an isotope of hydrogen in which the hydrogen atom has a neutron in its nucleus as well as a proton.

The heated gas is pumped to generators, where steam is produced. If light water is used, it may be allowed to boil, producing steam directly. This is called a direct steam cycle. If heavy water is used, it may heat a separate water supply. This is called an indirect steam cycle. The coolant is pumped back to the reactor after it has been used to heat the steam.

Moderators

A **moderator** is a substance that slows down neutrons so that they have a greater chance of striking fissile U235 nuclei. The moderator surrounds the fuel rods. It is generally a material such as graphite or heavy water.

Pressure vessels and shielding

The coolant in a nuclear reactor is kept under pressure, and for this reason the reactor core is surrounded by a pressure vessel.

It is of great importance that the people working in a nuclear power plant are shielded from harmful radiation. The pressure vessel gives some protection, but an additional shield is also required for most reactors. This is called the biological shield, or just simply "the shield." The shield has to be thick enough to protect the workers from neutrons and gamma radiation at all times. Concrete is a very good shielding material. Usually a thickness of about 7 to 10 feet (2 to 3 meters) surrounds the reactor.

CONTROL AND CONTAINMENT

Several steps are taken to ensure that radioactive materials stay within the reactor. The cladding keeps the fission products in the fuel rods. If they do escape, they will enter the coolant. The coolant flows in a closed loop around the reactor, and so fission products should not escape into the environment.

However, if there is a leak in the coolant circuit, then radioactivity will escape. The radioactivity will then reach another barrier to prevent it from spreading into the outside world. This next barrier is the reactor building itself, which is why it is called the reactor containment building.

Reactor control

The chain reactions in a nuclear reactor can be controlled by placing materials that absorb neutrons into the reactors. This is done by using control rods made of a neutron-absorber, such as boron or cadmium. These rods can be moved in and out of the reactor as needed. If the reactor is critical, meaning there is a continuous self-sustaining series of chain reactions in progress, it can be shut down (made "subcritical") by introducing control rods. The reactor can be started up again by simply removing the rods. The control rods need not be actual rods of material. Some reactors use a neutron-absorbing liquid or gas as part of their shutdown system.

■ Nuclear reactor control rods are inserted into the reactor core to absorb neutrons and to slow down chain reactions.

A reactor will typically have 50 or more control rods spread throughout the core. The operators of the power station will regulate the output of the reactor minute by minute by adjusting the positions of the rods. They move the rods in and out as the reactor is running to produce higher or lower levels of power output. The rate at which the fission process is taking place in the reactor core is determined by measuring the number of neutrons present in different parts of the reactor. The temperature and pressure of the coolant are also measured.

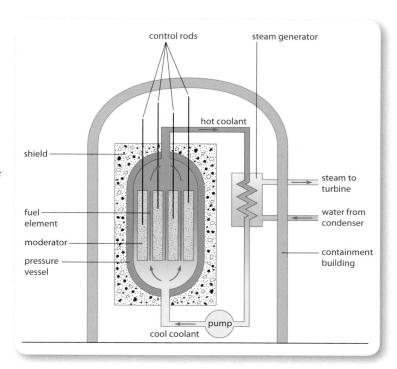

■ This is a cross-section of a reactor.

Shutdown rods

In addition to the control rods, a reactor is also equipped with shutdown rods. These are absorbers that are either kept out of the core (when the reactor is running) or in the core (when the reactor has been shut down). The shutdown rods are controlled independently and used to stop the chain reactions rapidly during an emergency.

Fission product heating

Even when the reactor has been shut down, it will still continue to produce heat. The chain reaction can be stopped by using control rods, but there is no way to stop the natural breakdown of the radioactive materials. This heat is called fission product heating. If steps are not taken to remove this heat, the fuel may melt. It is essential that the reactor core is cooled at all times, even when it is not producing energy. Emergency core-cooling systems are kept ready for use in case the main cooling system fails.

REACTOR SYSTEMS

There are several different types of nuclear power station around the world. Here, we will look at the more common types.

■ Dismantling an outdated Magnox reactor is a lengthy and dangerous process.

Advanced gas-cooled reactors (AGRs)

AGRs supply over half of the electricity produced by nuclear reactors in Great Britain. The AGR is the successor to the Magnox reactor, the first type to be built in Britain, in the 1960s. Magnox reactors produced low temperature steam and were rather inefficient. In May 2000 it was confirmed that all of Britain's Magnox reactors were to be shut down.

AGRs use enriched uranium dioxide as their fuel. This can be made into a ceramic. It has a melting temperature of over 3,632 °F (2,000 °C). As the name suggests, AGRs use gas (carbon dioxide) as their coolant. The core of an AGR is made from blocks of graphite through which cylindrical cooling channels are cut. The fuel elements are placed in these channels, and coolant flows through the channels. The heat output of an AGR is around 1,500 megawatts. From this, it produces 600 megawatts of electricity, making it about 40 percent efficient (600 being 40 percent of 1,500). This output is similar to that of a fossil fuel power station.

The pressure vessel is made of special concrete around 13 to 20 feet (4 to 6 meters) thick, with a thin lining of stainless steel to stop the coolant gas from escaping. After heating, the coolant gas is pumped to the steam generators, which are set in the walls of the concrete pressure vessel. Once the steam has been generated, the coolant is recycled to the reactor core. The steam produced goes to a steam turbine for electricity production.

Pressurized water reactors (PWRs)

PWRs are the most commonly used nuclear power stations in the world. They use normal water as both their coolant and their moderator. Because water absorbs neutrons, PWRs use enriched uranium.

The PWR uses uranium dioxide fuel rods clad in zirconium alloy, which resists corrosion by the water and does not absorb neutrons. The core of a PWR reactor is smaller than that of an AGR. Some of the fuel rods are left out to make room for the control and shutdown rods, which move up and down within the fuel elements. The whole core is enclosed by an 8-inch (20-centimeter) thick steel pressure vessel. PWRs have a heat output of about 3,000 megawatts and an electrical output of 1,000 megawatts.

The PWR has no cooling channels, and the fuel elements are packed closely together. The coolant passes up through the core between the fuel rods and is then pumped to a steam generator. After transferring its heat, the coolant is pumped back to the reactor. Each reactor has three or four of these cooling cycles.

To maintain a constant coolant pressure, there is a pressurizer. This has a pressure release valve in case the pressure gets too high. This is an essential part of the power station. If it goes wrong, it can be disastrous.

The reactor and the cooling systems are enclosed within a containment building with concrete walls about 3 feet (1 meter) thick. This is necessary because if the cooling system burst open, the high-pressure water inside would turn to steam instantly. This would cause a huge increase in pressure inside the building that could rupture the walls.

■ This is a PWR nuclear power station in California.

23

FAST BREEDERS, FAST MOVERS

Fast breeder reactors are used to produce new fissile material in the form of plutonium. A fast breeder reactor can produce as much fuel as it consumes. This is possible because when uranium 238 absorbs a neutron during the operation of a reactor, it is changed into plutonium 239. This is a fissionable isotope and can itself be used to fuel reactors.

A typical breeder reactor has an inner core, which is made up of a large number of stainless-steel tubes filled with a mixture of uranium oxide and plutonium oxide. This is surrounded by an outer blanket of tubes of natural uranium oxide. This breeding blanket, as it is called, captures neutrons that escape from the core, and the uranium is converted into plutonium. As in other reactors, heat is removed from the core by a liquid coolant and is used to produce steam. The steam powers a turbine that drives an electrical generator.

The core of a fast breeder reactor is very small because it has no moderator. A core 8 feet (2.5 meters) in diameter and 5 feet (1.5 meters) high will produce 1,000 megawatts of electricity. It also produces a great deal of heat—around three and a half times the output of a PWR. Liquid sodium is commonly used as a coolant. It transfers heat efficiently and, unlike water, does not readily absorb neutrons. The heat energy produced by the reactor core is so high that the fuel would melt in seconds if the coolant stopped flowing for any reason. As extra protection, the whole core is placed in a pool of liquid sodium into which heat can pass if the coolant system fails.

■ This is the reactor room at the Beloyarskaya fast breeder in Russia.

■ This experimental fast breeder reactor site is near Idaho Falls, Idaho.

Shutdowns

The world's first commercial fast breeder was the Superphénix, which was built in France. It began to produce electricity in 1986, but it has had many shutdowns since. The technology is controversial.

In the United States, many people are worried about the effects of plutonium on the environment. They also fear that it might fall into the hands of terrorists, who could use it to produce nuclear weapons. These fears have halted the development of breeder reactors. Congress cut off funding of breeder technology development in 1983. Great Britain shut down its prototype breeder reactor in 1994. Japan has continued its breeder program. In December 1995 its breeder, Monju, suffered a ruptured pipe in a secondary cooling system. This spilled an estimated 2 to 5 tons of liquid sodium, which then caught fire. The reactor is located 2,300 feet (700 meters) from an active earthquake fault.

NUCLEAR ENERGY ON THE MOVE

The U.S. Navy recognized the potential of nuclear power as an energy source. Under the direction of Hyman Rickover, a program to develop a naval reactor was launched in the late 1940s. In 1954 the first nuclear submarine, the *Nautilus*, was launched. It was a complete success. Today, many of the world's navies use nuclear-powered submarines. The *Nautilus* reactor was the prototype for the first U.S. commercial nuclear power plant, built in Shippingport, Pennsylvania, in 1957. The USS *Triton*, launched in 1959, is propelled by two nuclear reactors. In 1960 it traveled around the world underwater, covering 49,000 miles (78,858 kilometers) in 84 days.

SPENT FUEL AND REPROCESSING

Nuclear fuel lasts for about six years in a reactor. After it is removed, it is called spent fuel. This spent fuel consists of uranium, various isotopes of plutonium, and a variety of fission products. It is extremely dangerous because it is about 100 million times more radioactive than fresh fuel. Most of this radioactivity is due to the fission products that are themselves decaying and giving off radiation as they do so. There are two ways to deal with the spent fuel. It can either be stored or it can be reprocessed.

Reprocessing

After its removal from the reactor, spent fuel is stored in water ponds 33 feet (10 meters) deep on the reactor site. It is kept here for a year or so to allow some of the shorter-lived fission products to decay. This makes it slightly less dangerous for the workers who will handle it later. The water also cools the fuel. Some fission products leak through holes in the cladding and **contaminate** the surrounding water. The water itself then becomes low-level radioactive waste and needs to be disposed of.

The spent fuel has to be transported to a reprocessing plant. The safety of the flasks used to transport the fuel is a cause for concern to many. In one test, a flask was placed in front of a 155-ton locomotive traveling at 99 miles (160 kilometers) per hour. The flask remained intact. The first stage in reprocessing is to chop up the fuel rods and dissolve them in nitric acid. This

■ A flask for transporting spent nuclear fuel sits on a railroad car.

releases gaseous fission products, some of which have to be collected and disposed of. These, plus the fuel cladding, become an intermediate waste disposal problem.

The next stage is the separation of the uranium and plutonium from the fission products. A solution of the fission products then has to be stored as high-level waste. The uranium and plutonium are separated from each other. Nearly all of this material is stored. If uranium were to become scarce, this material could be used for reactor fuel at some point in the future.

Reprocessing and nuclear weapons

As we will see later, reprocessing is the link between nuclear reactors and nuclear weapons because it provides the plutonium for weapons manufacture. The United States banned commercial fuel reprocessing in the 1970s.

■ Storage cylinders containing uranium 238 are removed during the process of enriching unranium for nuclear fuel.

DEALING WITH NUCLEAR WASTE

One of the biggest difficulties for the nuclear industry is the question of what to do with radioactive waste. Low-level nuclear waste consists of materials such as contaminated clothing, packing material, and fittings from nuclear reactors. Intermediate-level wastes include fuel cladding and wastes from fuel reprocessing. These require more careful storage than low-level wastes.

Low-level nuclear wastes have been placed in concrete-lined ditches and covered with soil at waste sites. Controversially, liquid low-level wastes have simply been pumped into the sea. This has caused many large-scale protests.

High-level waste disposal

High-level waste includes spent fuel rods and fission products, such as plutonium. Spent fuel produces so much heat that it has to be cooled for decades, and it requires elaborate storage.

Disposing of wastes is different from storing them. Stored wastes are kept safe and accessible for up to 100 years for possible future treatment or use. Disposal means that the wastes are put safely out of reach, with no plans for their recovery. The current preference is to dispose of high-level waste by burying it in deep underground tunnels. The waste may or may not have been reprocessed.

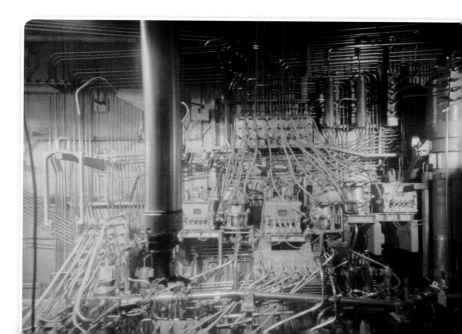

■ Spent nuclear fuel is encased in glass in the vitrification cell of a reprocessing plant.

■ The U.S. government plans to build a nuclear waste depository in Yucca Mountain, Nevada.

First, the waste is vitrified (encased in a special highly resistant glass). Next, cylinders of the vitrified waste are encased in 10-inch (25-centimeter) thick stainless steel containers. These containers can then be placed in underground shafts and tunnels between 1,000 and 3,300 feet (300 to 1,000 meters) deep. The tunnels are then backfilled with clay and other materials that prevent water from getting at the containers. The tunnel walls may also be lined with concrete as a further barrier. The final barrier is the hundreds of yards of rock between the depository and the surface.

Until such sites become a reality, nuclear power stations could simply become waste-holding facilities that store the contaminated remnants of their reactor plants, as well as the spent fuel. The U.S. Department of Energy was required to begin accepting spent nuclear fuel for disposal in January 1998, but it will be at least 2010 before its fuel burial site in Yucca Mountain, Nevada, is ready.

HOW LONG TO STORE?

It is very difficult to say how quickly radioactive wastes decay. There will be a range of different radioactive isotopes present, each with a different half-life, and each decaying into new radioactive isotopes that themselves will have different half-lives. Storing the wastes for ten years will reduce radioactivity significantly. The decay rate continues at a fast pace for between 100 and 1,000 years after the radioactive waste was formed. After that, the rate slows. Spent fuel has to be kept cooled for decades until the shorter half-life isotopes have decayed. It must be kept out of contact with the rest of the environment for hundreds of years, at the very least.

DISPOSAL DILEMMA

A major problem in disposing of nuclear waste lies in finding a suitable site. Most people do not want to live near a waste dump, especially a waste dump containing materials they believe to be harmful. No matter how much the industry or government might protest that the waste is safely locked away, people often still object.

■ A train-load of nuclear waste on its way to a disposal site passes the village of Seascale, in England.

Can we be certain?

Can scientists ever say with absolute certainty that a waste disposal site will remain secure over thousands of years? The answer would have to be no. Nuclear waste has to be kept isolated for 1,000 years at the very least, and it is very difficult to predict how conditions will change over such a long period. This makes assessing potential waste sites a particularly difficult task. For small countries with large numbers, there may be no acceptable sites for high-level waste disposal. Many people believe that, at present, we have no real solution to the problem of nuclear waste. It seems that, for the foreseeable future, vitrified high-level waste will be disposed of near the surface.

A wider problem

Of course, nuclear waste disposal is by no means the only disposal problem we have to face. We are rapidly running out of places to put new landfill sites for the millions of tons of household and industrial waste we generate. Many people believe that the haphazard "disposal" of carbon dioxide waste from fossil fuel power stations and other sources into the atmosphere is leading to global climate changes. We need to find ways to better manage hazardous wastes of all kinds.

To reprocess or not to reprocess?

Reprocessing nuclear waste actually creates an even larger volume of waste that has to be disposed of. An advantage of reprocessing is that it concentrates the dangerous high-level waste into a small volume. However, a major disadvantage is the large stockpiles of separated plutonium that it produces. There was some justification for reprocessing when the plutonium was going to be used to start fast breeder reactors, but this is no longer the case. Most fast-breeder programs have been cut back, postponed, or canceled. For many, the risks involved are a strong argument against reprocessing and for the long-term storage of spent fuel.

WASTE PRODUCTION

At each stage of reprocessing, wastes are produced. The reprocessing of 5.2 cubic yards (4 cubic meters) of spent fuel from a typical PWR reactor produces 3.3 cubic yards (2.5 cubic meters) of high-level waste, 52 cubic yards (40 cubic meters) of intermediate-level waste, and 785 cubic yards (600 cubic meters) of low-level waste. By contrast, a coal-fired power station with a similar power output leaves about 359,000 cubic feet (300,000 cubic meters) of ash that has to be disposed of.

■ Spent nuclear fuel from Japan arrives in Britain for reprocessing.

31

RADIATION AND LIFE

Radiation, which is silent, invisible, odorless, and potentially deadly, is something that we fear. Our senses give us no warning of the presence of radiation, which perhaps makes it even more frightening. So, what does radiation actually do to living things?

Ionizing radiation

Broadly speaking, radiation can be divided into two groups: electromagnetic radiation, which includes radio waves, visible light, X-rays, and gamma rays; and particle radiation, such as the neutrons, alpha particles, and beta particles given off by radioactive decay.

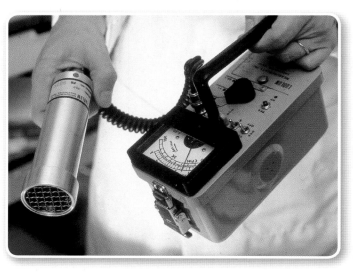

■ A Geiger counter is used to detect radioactivity.

Alpha and beta particles carry an electric charge. When alpha or beta particles pass through matter, the electrical forces between the particles and the electrons surrounding the atoms of the matter can be enough to push electrons from their orbits. This leaves the atom with a positive charge. This process is called ionization, and radiation that does this is called **ionizing radiation**.

Atoms are held together by bonds formed through sharing or transferring electrons. If electrons are removed by ionizing radiation, then these bonds are broken and new ones may be formed. If these chemical changes take place in a living organism, they can bring about biological changes that could be harmful. The amount of energy needed to cause damage to a living system is tiny. (For example, the amount of ionizing radiation needed to kill an adult human is equivalent to the energy needed to raise the body temperature by only 0.0045 °F, or 0.0025 °C.) It is the ionization and the disruption it causes to chemical processes that does the damage.

The effect on cells

Ionizing radiation can cause damage to any part of a living **cell**. However, damage to the cell nucleus tends to be more serious, because this is where the cell's DNA is found. DNA is like a chemical codebook carrying the instructions the cell needs to operate efficiently. If the cell's DNA is damaged, its activities will be disrupted and it may no longer be able to divide. This can have terrible effects, for example, on the cells that line the intestines. Here, cell division takes place continually as surface cells are generated to protect cells underneath. This protection will be lost if cell division stops.

Another possibility is that the damaged cell divides uncontrollably. This can result in cancer. Sometimes the damage done to the DNA may only become apparent if an affected person has children. All of the offspring's cells will carry the mutation that has been passed on by the parent. The vast majority of mutations are harmful and could result in miscarriage, stillbirth, or life-threatening birth defects.

Cells do have ways to repair the damage caused by ionizing radiation. For example, new DNA may be made to replace damaged strands. However, the repair methods can fail if there is a sudden, very large dose of radiation or if there are several doses separated by short periods of time.

■ Workers have to wear special protective radiation suits to carry out hazardous decontamination duties.

DOSAGE AND DAMAGE

■ Workers in the potentially dangerous environment of a nuclear power plant will wear "dosimeters" like this to monitor exposure to any radiation.

The type of radiation damage done to living animals depends on the type of radiation involved. Alpha particles are given off by elements such as uranium and plutonium. The range of an alpha particle is very short. It will not penetrate the outer skin layers, and it gives up its energy rapidly. Because they cause ionizing over a short distance, alpha particles are said to be densely ionizing. Damage is concentrated in a few cells, and the damage is difficult to repair. Alpha radiation particles are a serious danger if they get inside the body—for example, if uranium mine workers breathe in radioactive dust particles.

Beta particles are high-energy electrons and are more penetrating than alpha particles. The ionizing they produce is spread over a greater distance and so they are said to be lightly ionizing. The damage they cause can be more readily repaired.

Gamma radiation is highly penetrating, but only lightly ionizing. The ionization effect only occurs if the gamma rays strike atoms, causing them to send out electrons. Gamma rays are dangerous because they can penetrate deep into the body tissues, such as the bone marrow.

Safe levels?

It is extremely difficult to define a safe level of exposure to any potentially damaging substance, let alone radioactive ones. By "safe" do we mean no risk at all? This is just not practical, so we have to determine instead what level of risk is acceptable. This is another difficult task. Having done that, the next stage is to determine what level of radiation exposure matches the risk we are prepared to take. Again, this is not easy. At lower levels of exposure, the best we can do is to say that there is some chance of a fatal cancer resulting and that this risk increases with increasing exposure. What we cannot do is state with any confidence what the particular effect will be.

Working with radioactivity

Health officials have performed several large-scale studies of workers in the nuclear industry that show the effects of low-level radiation exposure. However, no clear link between the incidence of cancer in radiation workers and their exposure to low-level radiation has yet been established.

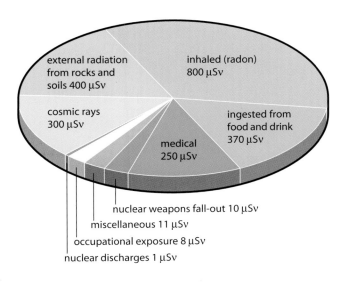

external radiation from rocks and soils 400 μSv

inhaled (radon) 800 μSv

cosmic rays 300 μSv

ingested from food and drink 370 μSv

medical 250 μSv

nuclear weapons fall-out 10 μSv

miscellaneous 11 μSv

occupational exposure 8 μSv

nuclear discharges 1 μSv

Radiation exposure is measured in sieverts (Sv). Humans can absorb 0.25 Sv without harmful effects. 1.5 Sv can produce radiation sickness. 8 Sv is fatal. This chart shows exposure for the average person from various sources in millionths (μ) of Sv.

SETTING THE LIMITS

Recommendations on radiation dose limits are set by the International Commission on Radiological Protection (ICRP). The basic principles applied by the ICRP are that no practice involving exposure to radiation should be adopted unless it produces an overall benefit to the population, and that all exposures to radiation should be **a**s **l**ow **a**s **r**easonably **p**ractical (the ALARP principle). How "overall benefit" and "reasonably practical" are defined is open to discussion. Those who oppose reprocessing, for example, claim it produces no overall benefit, and so radiation exposure from this procedure cannot be justified.

REACTOR ACCIDENTS

The biggest danger from nuclear power comes from exposure to radioactive materials. So far, major reactor accidents that release radioactivity into the environment have been rare. But it has happened, and it could happen again.

Windscale

In 1957 a fire broke out in the reactor at Windscale, in Cumbria, Great Britain. So far, it is the most serious accident to have occurred at a reactor in Britain.

On October 1, 1957, what had been a standard operating procedure went wrong. The temperature rose in the reactor and both the graphite moderator and the uranium fuel caught fire. Radioactive fission products were released into the atmosphere. As a result, milk from an area 190 square miles (500 square kilometers) around the site had to be destroyed to prevent radioactive iodine from entering the human **food chain**. None of the workers were exposed to levels high enough to cause radiation sickness, but they, and many people living nearby, received doses far greater than permitted levels. A full report of the accident was not made public until 1982, when a report issued by the National Radiological Protection Board suggested that an estimated 32 additional cancer deaths happened as a result of the contamination.

■ This is the nuclear power station at Three Mile Island, Pennsylvania.

Three Mile Island

On March 28, 1979, a pump circulating cooling water in one of two PWRs at Three Mile Island in Harrisburg, Pennsylvania, stopped operating. The coolant immediately began to heat up, and a few seconds later a pressure release valve in the pressurizer opened. Seconds after this, the reactor shutdown rods were deployed automatically and the chain reaction was stopped. Soon, the coolant temperature and pressure dropped, but the pressure relief valve stayed open.

The open valve allowed water to escape from the cooling circuit. It was eventually pumped into a storage tank from which fission products escaped into the environment. After two minutes, the falling coolant pressure triggered the emergency core cooling system. The operators, mistakenly thinking there was too much water in the core, turned the emergency cooling system off. Eventually the water in the primary cooling circuit started to boil, and the cladding on the fuel rods began to melt. Workers could not reestablish adequate cooling for sixteen hours. By that time, one-third of the fuel had melted and the containment building was contaminated. The reactor was never used again.

■ Workers at Three Mile Island practice retrieving items from a model of the damaged reactor.

EXPECTING THE UNEXPECTED

One problem that the mistakes at Three Mile Island made clear was that when accidents happen, workers may have no experience in dealing with them. Since accidents in nuclear power stations can be so incredibly dangerous, it is essential that they are dealt with efficiently. One answer is to use reactor simulators in training. A computer connected to a control panel simulates the behavior of the reactor under different circumstances, giving the operator the chance to learn how to deal with a variety of events.

CHERNOBYL AND BEYOND

The worst nuclear accident to date happened on April 26, 1986, to one of the reactors at Chernobyl, near the Ukranian town of Pripyat in the former Soviet Union. The Chernobyl reactor had been in operation since 1984 and was one of the Soviet Union's most successful nuclear power stations.

As part of a safety study, workers ran a test to determine how long the electricity generators would run if the steam supply to the turbine were cut off. During the test, the power level fell uncontrollably to a point where the reactor was becoming unstable. The reactor should have shut down automatically, but the operators prevented this. Despite the problems, they decided to go ahead with the test and shut off the steam supply to the turbines.

Out of control

At this point, only seven control rods were in the core, even though the operating instructions required a minimum of 30. The reactor became supercritical, and the control rods could not be inserted quickly enough to bring it under control. Within three to four seconds, the power rose to 100 times its maximum design level. Most of the core melted. A chemical explosion followed, as the melted fuel reacted with the cooling water and lifted the 2,200-ton reactor cap off. The building containing the reactor was blown apart. Fission products from the core were lifted high into the atmosphere by the hot gas and continued to stream out for ten days. By the time the fire was brought under control, radioactive material had spread across Europe.

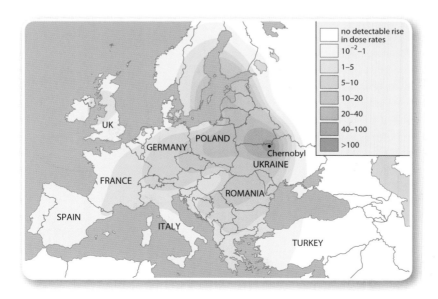

- Radiation levels rose across Europe after the Chernobyl disaster.

Russia today

Sosnovy-Bor, a suburb of St. Petersburg, has a digital Geiger counter on the town hall displaying local radiation levels in large red letters. The town's only industry is the Leningrad Nuclear Power Plant, a Chernobyl-type power station. Although the plant suffered a leak of radioactive material in 1992, it is currently being overhauled in order to extend its life for another fifteen years. Many organizations have expressed doubts about the safety of the plant. If Chernobyl had happened there, many of the four million people of St. Petersburg would have received a massive dose of radiation. The situation among

■ The massive damage caused by the explosion at Chernobyl is clear in this photo.

the workers gives cause for concern, too. Many employees do not wear any protective gear at all, and workers routinely get their government salaries as much as six months late.

Most experts agree that the only way to make the reactors safe is to shut them down. The U.S. Department of Energy has a list of the world's seven most dangerous reactors. All are in the former Soviet Union. In a 1995 report, the agency explained that many Soviet-designed reactors are still potential safety risks. These reactors continue to have serious incidents, which increases the likelihood of another accident similar to the one at Chernobyl.

COULD IT HAPPEN AGAIN?

Asked if he thought another Chernobyl could happen, a spokesman for the International Atomic Energy Agency said, "I don't think so. Safety has improved throughout the world. But there are no guarantees. And there's absolutely no reason for complacency. We have to do our best and cross our fingers." Does that sound reassuring?

NUCLEAR FUTURE

In the 1980s, orders for the building or starting up of nuclear reactors numbered between 20 to 40 per year. In 2004 there were just two orders for new construction (in Japan and India) and five orders for start-ups (in China, Japan, Ukraine, and Russia). It is money problems, not radiation dangers, that is bringing about the end of the nuclear power industry. As nuclear power plants age, it is becoming more expensive to maintain them. But because around 16 percent of the world's power now comes from nuclear plants, alternatives will have to be found.

The end of the nuclear dream?

During the course of its nuclear weapons production and energy research, the United States built 20,000 nuclear facitilities. Today, more than 5,000 of those facilities are unwanted or unused. In 1994 the U.S. Department of Energy inititated its National Deactivation and Decommissioning Program, which vowed to safely and economically remove these plants from service in a timely manner.

In 2004 this agency began a high-profile clean-up effort near Denver, Colorado. "Building 771" of the Rocky Flats Environmental Technology Site had once built nuclear weapons. Over the course of 50 years, the large plant developed a history of plutonium leaks and spills, and the media named it "the most dangerous building in America." When work began to demolish this dangerous site, many people saw this as an important step forward for the U.S. clean-up program.

Nuclear fusion

Nuclear **fusion** is the opposite of nuclear fission. Nuclear fusion occurs when the nuclei of two lighter atoms combine to form a heavier one, rather than a heavy nucleus splitting apart. The resulting atom has a smaller mass than the original ones, because some of the mass is transformed into energy.

This is the process that powers hydrogen bombs and stars. Gram for gram, fusion produces eight times more energy than the fission of uranium, and over a million times more than could be obtained by burning the same weight of fossil fuels. Fusion is not only desirable because it is such a wonderful energy source, but also because the fuels used (isotopes of hydrogen) are relatively abundant. Also, the product of the reaction is inert helium, rather than polluting gases or radioactive waste.

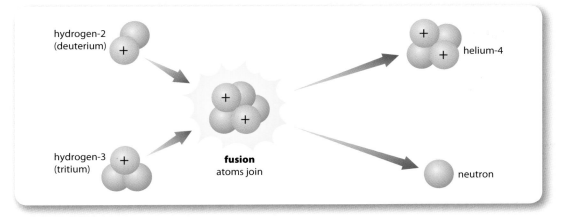

■ Two isotopes of hydrogen undergo fusion to become helium plus a neutron.

Research is being conducted into controlled fusion energy in many places, particularly the United States, Japan, and the European Union. However, in experiments so far, the energy obtained in the laboratory has scarcely exceeded the energy put in to run the tests. Fusion reactions are difficult to achieve because the nuclei have to be made to collide at very high speeds. This requires temperatures of 212 million °F (100 million °C) or more.

Few people believe that fusion power will be available commercially at any time in the foreseeable future. The extremely high cost of fusion research, and the uncertainty of a return on the investment, makes most businesses and governments very reluctant to finance its development. Cooperation among countries to share the costs may be the only way forward.

■ This nuclear fusion test reactor is at Princeton University.

NUCLEAR WEAPONS

There is no better illustration of the way people's ideas can be turned to a terrible purpose than nuclear weapons. The discovery that vast amounts of energy could be released by splitting the atom was an exciting one. It opened up the possibility of a new source of power for society. However, what spurred the effort to harness atomic power was not the desire to benefit society, but rather the desire to produce a bomb. The successful detonation of the first atomic bomb at Los Alamos, New Mexico, on July 16, 1945, began a new era. For decades to come, the threat of nuclear destruction would hang over Earth.

A bigger bang

In conventional explosives, a chemical reaction releases energy very rapidly. The amount of energy released depends on the mass of the explosive chemicals. Nuclear weapons are different, but the energy they release is often given in terms of the equivalent amount of TNT, a common explosive, needed to produce the same results.

A fission weapon contains pure, or nearly pure, plutonium 239 or uranium enriched to over 90 percent U235. Around the outside of the bomb is a layer of conventional explosives. When the explosives are triggered, the fissile material is compressed, making it supercritical and bringing about a runaway chain reaction within millionths of a second.

■ A U.S. soldier surveys the devastation caused by the atomic bomb at Hiroshima.

A fusion weapon uses the power of a fission bomb to provide the energy needed to heat up and compress isotopes of hydrogen so that they fuse together and give off dangerous amounts of energy. Because fusion weapons use hydrogen, they are often referred to as hydrogen bombs, or H bombs.

Weapons production

If a country wants to build nuclear weapons, it needs a supply of fissile material. This means having either a uranium enrichment facility or a nuclear reactor to produce plutonium and a reprocessing plant to extract it. The amount of plutonium needed to make a weapon varies, but 22 pounds (10 kilograms) is average. Quite small reactors, not designed to produce electricity, can be used for weapons production.

The International Atomic Energy Agency monitors the use of nuclear technology to make sure that it is only used for peaceful purposes. It sometimes sends inspectors to countries to make sure that they are not building nuclear weapons. Today, many countries are concerned that Iran and North Korea may be using their nuclear technology to develop weapons.

■ Tension between India and Pakistan grew in 1998 when India conducted five underground nuclear weapons tests near the Pakistan border.

TIMELINE

1896 French physicist Antoine Henri Becquerel discovers radioactivity

1905 Albert Einstein shows that mass and energy can be converted from one to the other

1919 New Zealand physicist Ernest Rutherford splits the atom by bombarding a nitrogen nucleus with alpha particles

1939 Otto Hahn, Fritz Strassmann, and Lise Meitner announce the discovery of nuclear fission

1942 Enrico Fermi builds the first nuclear reactor in a squash court at the University of Chicago

1945 The first atom bomb is detonated at Los Alamos, New Mexico

1951 The experimental fast breeder reactor, near Idaho Falls, Idaho, produces the first electricity to be generated by nuclear energy

1956 The world's first commercial nuclear power station, Calder Hall, comes into operation in the United Kingdom

1957 In Kyshtym, USSR (now Russia), the escape of plutonium waste causes an unknown number of casualties. On maps produced the following year, 30 small communities are erased. Radiation is released from Windscale (now Sellafield) nuclear power station in Cumbria, England.

1979 A nuclear-reactor accident occurs at Three Mile Island, Pennsylvania

1986 An explosion in a reactor at Chernobyl, Ukraine, results in clouds of radioactive material spreading across Europe as far as Sweden

1991 The first controlled production of nuclear-fusion energy is achieved at the Joint European Torus (JET) in Culham, England

1995 Sizewell B, the most advanced nuclear power station in the world, begins operating in Suffolk, England

1997 English physicists at JET produce a record 12 megawatts of nuclear-fusion power

1999 Japan's worst-ever nuclear accident results in 49 people, mostly plant workers, being exposed to potentially harmful levels of radiation

2006 The first generation of nuclear reactors are coming to the end of their life and are being decommissioned. Will governments build a new generation of reactors, or will we have to find the energy from somewhere else?

INTERNATIONAL NUCLEAR EVENT SCALE

The International Nuclear Event Scale (INES) was designed to communicate to the public the safety issues of reported events at nuclear installations. There are seven levels, with level 7 the most dangerous.

7 Major accident
Example: Chernobyl, USSR (now Ukraine), 1986

6 Serious accident
Example: Kyshtym Reprocessing Plant, USSR (now Russia), 1957

5 Accident with off-site risk
Examples: Windscale Pile, UK, 1957; Three Mile Island, U.S., 1979

4 Accident without significant off-site risk
Windscale Reprocessing Plant, UK, 1973; Saint-Laurent NPP, France, 1980; Buenos Aires Critical Assembly, Argentina, 1983

3 Serious incident
Example: Vandellos NPP, Spain, 1989

2 Incident

FIND OUT MORE

If you want to learn more about nuclear energy, there is plenty of information on the Internet and in books . Use a search engine such as www.google.com to search for information. A search for the words *nuclear energy* will bring back lots of results, but it may be difficult to find the information you want. Try refining your search to look for some of the people and things mentioned in this book, such as "Albert Einstein" or "Chernobyl."

More Books to Read

Fullick, Ann. *Turning Up the Heat: Energy*. Chicago: Heinemann Library, 2005.

McLeish, Ewan. *Energy Resources*. Chicago: Raintree, 2002.

Saunders, Nigel, and Steven Chapman. *Nuclear Energy*. Chicago: Raintree, 2005.

GLOSSARY

alpha particle   positively charged, high energy particle consisting of two protons and two neutrons given off from the nucleus of a radioactive atom. Releasing an alpha particle transforms one element into another as the atomic number is reduced by two.

atom   smallest unit of matter that can take part in a chemical reaction. Also, the smallest part of an element that can exist.

atomic energy   *see* nuclear energy

atomic number   number of protons in the nucleus of an atom. Every element has a different atomic number.

beta particle   electron ejected at high speed from the nucleus of a radioactive atom; created when a neutron changes into a proton, giving off an electron as it does so

boron   chemical element used in the making of control rods for nuclear reactors because of its ability to absorb neutrons

cell   smallest unit of life capable of independent existence. All living things, with the exception of viruses, consist of one or more cells.

chain reaction   fission reaction in which neutrons released by the splitting of atomic nuclei strike other nuclei, causing them to split and release more neutrons. This causes still more nuclei to split, and so on.

chemical energy   energy held in the bonds that hold atoms together in molecules. Chemical energy is released during a chemical reaction.

cladding   metal covering around a rod or pellet of nuclear fuel

contaminate   to make impure by adding unwanted or undesirable substances

coolant   chemical designed to cool something down

decay   disintegration of the nuclei of radioactive elements

diffuse   to mingle with another substance through the movement of particles

electron   one of the subatomic particles that make up an atom. Electrons have a negative electric charge and orbit around the central nucleus of the atom.

element   substance that cannot be split into a simpler substance by means of a chemical reaction

fissile material   element that will break apart, or fission, when struck by a neutron

fission   splitting of a large atomic nucleus into two or more smaller nuclei

food chain   feeding pathway by which energy and mass is passed from one living organism to another

fossil fuel   fuel produced through the action of heat and pressure on the fossil remains of plants and animals that lived millions of years ago. Fossil fuels include coal, petroleum, and natural gas.

fuel rod   rod or pellet of fissile material, usually uranium, together with its protective cladding, used to power a nuclear reactor

fusion   process by which two small atomic nuclei combine to produce a single larger nucleus, with the release of a great deal of energy

gamma radiation   high-energy, short-wavelength electromagnetic radiation released from a radioactive atom

half-life   time it takes for half of a quantity of a radioactive substance to decay. Half-lives can vary from billionths of a second to billions of years.

heat energy energy associated with the motion of atoms and molecules

ionizing radiation radiation that knocks electrons from atoms, leaving positively charged ions in its path

isotopes atoms that have the same number of protons (and are therefore of the same chemical element) but have different numbers of neutrons, and so have different atomic masses

kinetic energy energy of movement

mass amount of matter in an object

meltdown accident in a nuclear reactor in which the reactor core melts as a result of the fuel overheating

moderator material used in a nuclear reactor to reduce the speed of high-energy neutrons and so control the rate at which energy is produced

molecule two or more atoms joined together by chemical bonds. If the atoms are the same, it is an element; if they are different, it is a compound.

neutron one of the subatomic particles that make up an atom. Neutrons have no electric charge and are found in the central nucleus of the atom.

nuclear energy (also called atomic energy) energy in the nucleus of an atom released when a large nucleus breaks down into two smaller nuclei (fission) or when two small nuclei combine to form a larger nucleus (fusion)

nucleus central part of an atom, made up of protons and neutrons and containing nearly all of the atom's mass

oxide compound that contains oxygen

porous capable of having liquids and other substances pass through it

proton one of the subatomic particles that make up an atom. Protons are in the central nucleus of the atom and have a positive electric charge.

radiation energy given off in the form of fast-moving particles or electromagnetic waves as a result of the decay of an atomic nucleus

radioactive describes a substance that gives off radiation

radioactivity release of radiation from a substance in the forms of alpha and beta particles and gamma rays

reactor structure in which radioactive material is made to break down in a controlled way, releasing energy that can be put to use

turbine engine in which a fluid is used to spin a shaft by pushing on angled blades like those on a fan. Turbines are used to spin generators that produce electricity.

INDEX

DATE DUE			